EXPRESS yourself

A HAND LETTERING workbook

FOR KIDS!

CREATE AWESOME QUOTES THE FUN AND EASY WAY!

EXPRESS yourself

A HAND LETTERING workbook

FOR KIDS!

CREATE AWESOME QUOTES THE FUN AND EASY WAY!

Amy Latta

PAGE STREET
PUBLISHING CO.

PAGE STREET
PUBLISHING CO.

First published in 2018 by
Page Street Publishing Co.
27 Congress Street, Suite 105
Salem, MA 01970
www.pagestreetpublishing.com

Distributed by Macmillan, sales in Canada by The Canadian Manda Group.

22 21 20 19 18   1 2 3 4 5

ISBN-13: 978-1-62414-613-8
ISBN-10: 1-62414-613-9

Library of Congress Control Number: 2018936865

Book design by Page Street Publishing Co.
Illustrations and cover design by Amy Latta

Printed and bound in China

Page Street Publishing protects our planet by donating to nonprofits like The Trustees, which focuses on local land conservation.

FOR NATHAN AND NOAH,
MY FAVORITE KIDS ON THE PLANET.

I LOVE YOU MORE.

CONTENTS

INTRODUCTION

Hi, there! I'm Amy, and I think you and I have something in common. We both enjoy creating art. I love to create all kinds of crafts and DIY projects, but my absolute favorite art form is hand lettering, and I can't wait to teach you all about it. Hand lettering has gotten really popular in the last few years and, believe it or not, it's something that anyone can do.

Once you learn the basics, you'll want to letter everything . . . and you can! In fact, the final chapter (page 140) of this book has five simple project ideas and a long list of other ways to use your new hobby. I also have lots of lettering tutorials and practice sheets available on my blog at www.oneartsymama.com, so be sure to check those out sometime.

Now, let's get started! I can't wait to show you how to create fabulous and unique hand lettered art.

Amy Latta

HOW TO USE THIS BOOK

Hand lettering is a huge topic. There are more fonts, doodles and tips than anyone could possibly fit into one book. Rather than trying to learn everything at once, we're going to start from the beginning and take things one step at a time. There are twenty chapters for you to go through at your own pace. Each one will teach you a new lettering style, doodle or skill that you can use to create awesome hand lettered art. You'll get step-by-step instructions as well as space to practice right here in the book. You can also have a separate sketchbook handy in case you want to continue practicing even more.

Each chapter features a sample design based on a popular quote. We'll talk a little about the quote and what it means and then, at the end of the chapter, there's a special page where you can recreate that sample design using the new skills you learned. The page is blank in the center for your artwork and has a hand-drawn border around the edges that you can color in if you like. When you're finished with the book, you can always cut out your work and put it on display. You can also photograph or scan your art and share it online or print it out to frame.

Are you ready? Let's get creative!

SUPPLY LIST

There are many different supplies that can be used for hand lettering. Here's a list of what you'll definitely need to get started, along with some extra things you might want to pick up as you get further into the book. All of these supplies can be found online or in your favorite craft and hobby store.

FOR BASIC LETTERING

- Pencil

- Eraser: I use the Tombow Mono eraser

- Ruler or other straightedge

- Markers: I like using Tombow TwinTones for colors and Tombow Mono Drawing Pens for black, but any markers will do

- Sketchbook (optional): I recommend one with medium weight paper (60 to 80 lb) that is as smooth as possible

FOR THE WATERCOLOR TECHNIQUE (CHAPTERS 6–20)

- Water pen: I like the Pentel Arts Aquash or Martha Stewart water pens

- Tombow Dual Brush Pens: these come in 96 colors and are usually sold in sets of 10

- Nonabsorbent surface: I use a plastic sandwich bag or a laminated piece of cardstock

- Hot-press watercolor paper (for more practice): this type of paper gives the best results because it's smooth and designed not to curl when wet

FOR BRUSH LETTERING (CHAPTER 17)

- Brush tip marker: I recommend the Tombow Fudenosuke or Tombow Dual Brush Pens

FOR GALAXY LETTERING (CHAPTER 19)

- Supplies used for the watercolor technique (above)

- White gel pen: I like the Sakura Gelly Roll

You can find a full list of all my favorite lettering and crafting supplies at www.amazon.com/shop/oneartsymama.

MASTERING FAUX CALLIGRAPHY SCRIPT

you've got this

Do you want to know what I love most about art? Art is never wrong. Unlike a math problem that has one correct answer, art is open-ended. You can create anything you can imagine. As we work through the lessons in this book together, remember that even when something you write turns out different from what you expected, it's still awesome. Your art should be your own and reflect your personality and style. Some of the lessons will be easy for you, while others might take practice and patience, but you've got this. You're already on your way to creating amazing things!

The art of hand lettering actually includes many different styles of writing, as well as embellishments and doodles. Basically, it's all about creating awesome-looking artistic designs that are focused on written words, no matter how you choose to do it. There is one particular writing style, though, that's become incredibly popular, and it's the main thing most people associate with hand lettering. It's called brush script, and it's basically cursive writing that has letters made with a mixture of thick and thin lines. The technique behind brush lettering is to use a special brush pen and control the thickness of the lines by the amount of pressure you put on the pen.

Later in the book, we'll learn and practice that technique a bit to give you a feel for how it works. Honestly, it's a little tricky to do, and it will take a lot of practice and repetition before you'll get the hang of it, so instead of starting with the authentic technique, we're going to begin our lettering lessons with the next best thing: faux calligraphy. Faux calligraphy looks very similar to brush script, but it's much easier to do! You'll be a pro at it in no time, and you'll be able to write anything and everything you want in a fabulous hand lettered style. Ready to get started?

FAUX CALLIGRAPHY SCRIPT
STEP 1
Write your word in cursive.

You'll want to leave just a little bit more space in between the letters than you normally would. You can use any type of pen, marker or even a pencil to try this technique.

STEP 2

Find your downstrokes and draw a second line for each one.

What's a downstroke? Every time you write, your pen is either moving up, down or horizontally across the page. A downstroke is any time your pen moves down toward you on the paper. The trick to getting the look we want is to draw thick downstrokes and keep all the upstrokes and horizontal strokes thin. In the example below, you can see how I have a second line only where the pen was moving down on the paper as I wrote my word.

you've

STEP 3

Color in the double line areas to give them the appearance of thick lines.

you've

That's all there is to it! Now you have that pretty brush lettered look with a contrast between thick and thin lines in your letters. It's actually really easy to do, right? For most people, the hardest part is figuring out exactly where the downstrokes are in a specific word or letter. To help you as you're practicing, here is a sample alphabet for you to look at while you write. It's okay if you form some of your cursive letters differently than I do. You want to have your own unique style! This is just a reference to help you figure out which lines should be thick and which stay thin.

abcdefghij
klmnopqr
stuvwxyz

In the practice space on the next page, use these letters as a guide as you try writing some words like *joy*, *love*, your name and, of course, the words in this design.

joy love

When you're ready, create your masterpiece in the special bordered space on the next page. You might want to sketch your phrase in pencil first to get it centered and spaced where you want it to go before tracing over it with a marker. Drawing horizontal lines on the page with a ruler or other straightedge before you start will help you keep your letters lined up. Once your design is finished, you can cut the page out of this book, take a photo of it or scan it into a computer. Then you'll be able to print it out, frame it or share it online.

PRACTICE BELOW

TWO

EMBELLISHING WITH FANCY FLOURISHES

Imagine you were granted one wish to change something about yourself. Most of us wouldn't have to think too hard to come up with what it would be. Magazines and movie stars can make us feel like we need to be thinner, prettier or more popular. Some of us might want to be funnier, more athletic or smarter. But guess what? You don't need to change a single thing. You're enough just the way you are. If you ask the people who matter most—your parents, your best friends and your mentors—they'll say the same thing. They don't love you for how you look or how fast you can run a mile. Those things don't make you valuable; it's the real you they care about. Next time you look in the mirror, instead of focusing on what you want to change, remind yourself that you are already enough.

Sometimes, a word or phrase written in Faux Calligraphy Script (page 11) can stand alone and look fantastic. Other times, you might want to add a few extra decorations to take your artwork to the next level. One easy way to embellish your lettering is with some basic flourishes. They're simple to draw, but they make a big difference in how your project looks. We're going to take a look at a few different types and then you can use your favorites to accent your designs.

The specific design we'll be creating in this chapter is meant to help you remember that you are enough, just the way you are. In addition to creating it here in your book, you might also want to make a copy to hang on your mirror or in your locker as a daily reminder.

FANCY FLOURISHES

The easiest flourish to create is a simple swirl. If you can draw a spiral, you can create these embellishments. All you have to do is draw a spiral and then give it a tail that's as long or short as you like.

These swirls work well all by themselves, or you can draw them in pairs.

Here's how it looks when you put a spiral on both ends. This looks great as a border or as a way to underline an important word.

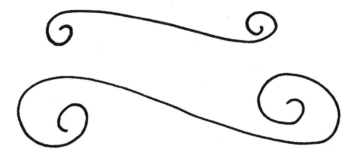

Another type of flourish I use a lot is really just a curving line with a little loop added on. You can make the loop go up or down, depending on what works best with your design.

Once again, these flourishes can stand alone, or you can pair them together and make your design symmetrical (the same on both sides).

In the space below, take some time to practice the swirls and looping flourishes. Play around with making them different lengths, colors and styles. I think you'll find that these are fun to use and really add a lot to your lettering.

When you're ready to create your design, pencil in the quote "you are enough" on the border page. Don't forget that you'll get a better result by first sketching the horizontal pencil lines so your words are straight and centered. Then sketch your favorite flourishes around the words. Once you're happy with your design, go back over it with markers to create your Faux Calligraphy Script (page 11), and erase any pencil lines you can still see.

PRACTICE BELOW

THREE

FUNKY PRINT FONT

One of the best things about human beings is that no two of us are exactly alike, not even identical twins. In a world of over 7.5 billion people, not one of them is just like you! Sometimes, though, we forget what a great thing that is. Instead of celebrating our individuality, we get focused on trying to fit in and be just like everyone else. Each of us has something special to offer. We all have different talents, personalities and interests for a reason. If everyone were the same, just think how boring the world would be. Instead of blending in with the crowd, let people see what makes you unique! As Dr. Seuss said, "Why fit in when you were born to stand out?" Take your special traits and let them shine for everyone to see!

We all know how to print. In fact, it's the first way we learn to write. But did you know that printing is actually really useful in hand lettered designs? As great as our Faux Calligraphy looks, it's not always meant to stand alone. When we want to letter a longer quote or phrase, it's better to mix things up and use a combination of print and script to make our design more interesting and help people focus on the most important words. Although you can certainly use your regular printing, it's fun to make the printed letters more artistic too. In this chapter we're going to learn the quick and easy Funky Print Font that pairs perfectly with the Faux Calligraphy you already know. Let's get started!

FUNKY PRINT FONT

When we write, we use certain guidelines to show us where the different parts of our letters go. Sometimes, the guidelines are visible, like the lines on notebook paper; other times, we can't see any guidelines at all. Even if we aren't consciously thinking about them, they're in the back of our brains, left over from when we first learned to write, and they affect the way our letters come out on paper. Here's a look at where the guidelines are and what they tell us.

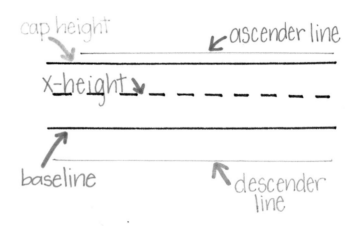

The baseline is the line our letters sit on. It's where the bottom of each letter begins and ends, unless the letter has a tail called a descender, like a lowercase *g*, *j* or *p*. Those tails go all the way down past the baseline to what's called the descender line. The cap height line shows us how tall our capital letters should be. The x-height shows how tall our lowercase letters should be, except for letters like *t*, *d* and *b* that go all the way up to the ascender line. X-height is where we draw those horizontal lines called crossbars that go across letters like *t* and *f*.

Normally, the x-height line is between the cap height and the baseline, a little higher than the center. As artists, though, we can play around with things like that to change the look of our letters. One easy way to make our normal printing look totally different and funky (in a good way!) is to place the crossbars in a different spot instead of at the x-height. In this chapter we're going to look at an alphabet that places them much lower, just above the baseline. To form these letters, all we do is print as we normally would, but we cross our letters close to the bottom, like this.

Also, we'll make the curved lines of letters like *R* and *P* touch their stem close to the baseline instead of higher up like we normally do.

Here's a look at the upper and lowercase alphabet written in this style, which we're going to call the Funky Print Font.

ABCDEFGHIJKLMNO
PQRSTUVWXYZ

abcdefghijklmno
pqrstuvwxyz

In the practice space below, take some time to write individual letters and words using this new style. Then use it along with your Faux Calligraphy Script (page 11) and flourishes (page 17) to letter the Dr. Seuss quote on the border page. You'll want to start by penciling in horizontal lines for your baselines and any other guidelines you'd like to use. Then pencil in your words and go back over them with markers to create your final design.

PRACTICE BELOW

FOUR

DRAWING DONUTS

Before Thomas Edison invented a light bulb that worked, he made 1,000 that didn't! I'm sure there were plenty of times he felt like quitting. Wouldn't you? But thank goodness he didn't, or we might still be living in the dark. It's no fun to fail even one time, let alone 1,000, but if we give up, we'll never know what we could have done. There are plenty of successful people whose lives tell the same story. Walt Disney went bankrupt before he created the Walt Disney Company. Michael Jordan was cut from his high school basketball team before becoming one of the best NBA players ever. We all fail sometimes, but it's what we choose to do next that matters. If you want your dreams to become reality, don't ever give up. Your light bulb moment might be just one more try away.

No matter who you are or where you're from, we have something in common. We all have to eat! And I'm betting that we just might have some of the same favorite foods. As delicious as they are, our favorite foods aren't just for eating. We can also learn to doodle them so that they can make our hand lettered designs even more awesome. In this chapter we're going to look at one particular food item that I'm pretty sure you like as much as I do—donuts! You'll learn to sketch a basic donut, then you can change the "flavor" by the way you choose to color it.

In this chapter our lettering project is going to remind us that we can do anything we put our minds to if we "donut ever give up."

BASIC DONUTS

STEP 1

Draw a circle.

Don't worry if it's not perfectly round. Whenever something is created by hand, there will be little imperfections. It's all part of the hand-drawn look, so embrace it instead of getting frustrated.

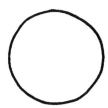

STEP 2

Draw a smaller circle inside.

Think about how a real donut looks. Make sure your inner circle isn't too big, or there won't be enough to your donut—although I would like to eat a giant munchkin!

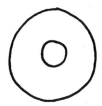

STEP 3

Draw a wavy line around the inside of the big circle.

This will be the edge of your icing.

STEP 4

Color in your donut and icing.

Here's where you get to be creative. A light tan or golden color is good for the donut itself and then you can choose your favorite frosting: chocolate, strawberry, vanilla or any other color of the rainbow.

STEP 5

Add sprinkles!

Use fine-tip pens or markers of many colors to draw short, colorful lines or dots that represent sprinkles. If you chose to use dark brown for chocolate icing, you may want to use gel pens because the ink in a gel pen sits on top of the paper and will show up better than regular pens or markers will.

Have a different favorite food? Here are some other easy illustrations and funny food puns you can have fun with and that your friends will love!

YOU'RE SO *sweet*

LET'S *taco* BOUT IT !

I'M KIND OF A BIG *dill*...

YOU'LL ALWAYS HAVE A "*pizza*" MY HEART...

YOU'RE "*avo*" CONTROL

In the practice space below, it's time to get busy making some donuts. Try a variety of sizes and colors, and you can even try some without holes to represent the kinds that are filled with jelly or cream. Also, try your hand at drawing some of the other food examples or even experimenting with your own food designs!

When you're ready, go on over to the border page to sketch our "donut ever give up" quote in a mixture of Faux Calligraphy Script (page 11) and Funky Print Font (page 22) and accent it with whatever kinds of donuts you like best. There are lots of other donut quotes you can create too, like "donut worry, be happy" or "donut go breaking my heart," that are fun to draw on cards for your friends.

PRACTICE BELOW

FIVE

FAUX CALLIGRAPHY PRINT

WORK hard and BE kind

Every day, you make hundreds of decisions. Will you get out of bed or will you snooze? Will you do your homework or not? No matter how hard it might be, there are certain things that are always the right choice. It's always better to work hard rather than not to give your best effort. You'll never regret giving something your best shot. You'll also never regret choosing to be kind. It may be hard right now to be nice to the girl or boy everyone else makes fun of, but it says a lot about who you are. Being kind to everyone, no matter how different they are from you, is another thing you'll always be glad you did. These kinds of choices make you the person you are and will put you on the right path every time. What do you have to do today that deserves your very best effort? Who needs a smile and a kind word from you?

Now that you're an expert at writing in Faux Calligraphy Script (page 11) and Funky Print Font (page 22), we can take those same basic skills and use them to create a Calligraphy Print alphabet too! The more styles of writing you can do, the more choices you have when you're designing a project, and that's always a good thing. Using two or three fonts to letter one quote makes it more interesting to look at and helps us emphasize the most important words. This Faux Calligraphy Print combines well with both of the other fonts you've learned and is definitely more interesting than normal, everyday printing.

Let's get to work learning our newest lettering style so we can create a visual reminder of the important choices to work hard and be kind. This would be a great phrase to display in your room or in your locker at school, where you will see it every day.

FAUX CALLIGRAPHY PRINT

Just like our Faux Calligraphy Script (page 11), Faux Calligraphy Print is made up of both thick and thin lines. Once again, we're going to look for our downstrokes and make them thicker than our upstrokes and horizontal lines, but this time we're thickening just the first downstroke of each letter.

STEP 1

Print your word.
Make sure to leave a little bit of extra space in between each letter.

STEP 2

Draw a double line next to the first downstroke of each letter.

Remember that downstrokes are all the lines that you draw with your pen moving down toward yourself (see page 13 for a refresher if you need it).

STEP 3

Color in the space between the double lines.

See? It's easy! You already know everything you need to write in this style.

Here's a sample uppercase and lowercase alphabet you can refer to that will help you figure out which lines are thick and which ones are thin.

Aa Bb Cc Dd Ee Ff
Gg Hh Ii Jj Kk Ll Mm
Nn Oo Pp Qq Rr Ss Tt
Uu Vv Ww Xx Yy Zz

Using the sample alphabet as a guide, practice your Faux Calligraphy Print letters on the next page or in a separate sketchbook. I think you'll find that this style comes easily since you've already got the hang of the basic technique. Then when you're ready, sketch and color your quote design on the border page. You'll want to begin by penciling in two horizontal lines. Next, sketch your word placement, paying attention to which letter or space is the center of each line. I like to draw the center letter first and then work my way out to the sides. When you have the spacing the way you want it, use your markers to letter the words in a combination of the styles you've learned, along with some pretty swirls (page 17). Feel free to use the sample as a guide or to use whatever mix of font styles you like best.

PRACTICE BELOW

EXPRESS YOURSELF: A HAND LETTERING WORKBOOK FOR KIDS!

SIX

WATERCOLOR WITHOUT PAINT

When I was in high school, I earned a trip to Memphis, Tennesee, through the 4-H program. I had worked hard for it, but I ended up not going because I was afraid to fly. My friends came back with stories about the wonderful time they had, and I'd spent the whole weekend bored at home. I knew then that I didn't want to let any more adventures slip away. Years later, I did visit Memphis, and guess what? It's awesome. I saw ducks swimming in the fountain at the Peabody Hotel and toured Sun Studios where Elvis Presley recorded some of his music. I also stuffed my face with the world's best BBQ nachos. It was an adventure, and I loved every minute of it. There are lots of adventures in store for you too. Some might involve travel, or they might involve trying a new sport, joining a club or meeting a new friend. Don't let your fears hold you back. The adventure might be scary or intimidating, but it's worth taking the risk. Trust me; Memphis would have been way better than sitting around in my room with no nachos!

Our "adventure awaits" design is going to be a colorful one, so let's jump in and find out how to make it look awesome using a supercool technique.

The way a design is colored can be just as important as how we choose to letter it. Of course, you can always use whatever supplies you happen to have on hand. Colored pencils, markers and even crayons will work just fine to add color to your projects. One of my favorite ways to color a design, though, is with a watercolor technique that doesn't require any paint! You get the look of a pretty watercolor painting without the mess, and it's easy to do just about anywhere. Personally, I love this effect because it gives your image a softer look and gets rid of the streaks you sometimes have when you color something with markers. In this chapter we'll take a look at how it works and then you can use it throughout the book to add color to your lettered quotes as well as the border page illustrations.

WATERCOLOR WITHOUT PAINT

You might be wondering how in the world we're going to watercolor without actually using any paint. What do we use instead? All you need are water-based markers (I recommend Tombow Dual Brush Pens), a water pen and a nonabsorbent surface. For the surface, you can use anything from a plastic sandwich bag to a laminated piece of cardstock. In a pinch, I've been known to use a trash bag or even the lid from a plastic container of potato salad! It just has to be something with a shiny coating so that when you color on it with your marker, the ink pools up and sits on top instead of getting absorbed as it would on paper.

Water pens are like paintbrushes, but their handles are filled with water so the tip is constantly wet. You can find water pens at your local craft store or online at sites like Amazon or blitsy.com. My favorites are the Pentel Aquash pens or the Martha Stewart Water Brushes. Once you've gathered your supplies, turn the page to learn what you'll do.

STEP 1

Sketch a shape you'd like to color in.

A simple triangle with a straight vertical line through the center makes a basic pine tree like the ones in my sample design. Be sure to use a non-water-based marker for the outline.

STEP 2

Scribble with any color water-based marker(s) you want to use on the nonabsorbent surface.

Don't worry about being neat. The goal is to get ink onto the surface so you can use it.

STEP 3

Dip the tip of your water pen into the ink.

Make sure you have filled the barrel of the pen with clean water first. As you dip the brush into the ink, you should see the tip of the brush start to take on the ink's color.

STEP 4

Use the water pen like a paintbrush and fill in the blank areas of your design.

That's all there is to it! The water pen is self-cleaning, so as it runs out of ink, the brush will turn clear again. You can reload it with more of the same color or pick up a new color instead. If you want to change colors before you've run out of the first one, just move the water pen back and forth on a paper towel or a scrap piece of paper until it goes clear.

One of the best things about this technique is how easy it is to blend colors. All you have to do is rub the pen into several different colors instead of just one, and they'll mix together as you paint! I have a feeling this is one of those things you're going to want to practice a lot because it's so easy and so much fun. You might find yourself wanting to watercolor everything. I sure do!

Take some time in the practice space on the next page or in a separate sketchbook to play around with this watercolor technique. Then you can use it to color in the quote design you're going to draw on the border page. First you're going to use the Faux Calligraphy Script (page 11) to letter "adventure awaits." Then pencil in a horizontal line with a triangle on one end and a series of *v* shapes on the other to make an arrow. Finally, sketch whatever kind of scene you think of when it comes to adventure. It could be simple triangles for mountains and trees, a map or anything that has to do with travel. Then use your new watercolor technique to color in your illustrations.

If you like this technique and want to do more practice and projects, I recommend getting a pad of hot-press watercolor paper. First of all, watercolor paper is specifically designed to work well when wet and won't curl or distort like regular sketch paper does. Unlike cold-press watercolor paper, which has a rough texture, hot-press paper is very smooth and won't cause your lettering to look bumpy.

PRACTICE BELOW

EXPRESS YOURSELF: A HAND LETTERING WORKBOOK FOR KIDS!

SEVEN

POLKA DOT-FILLED ALPHABET

Nobody likes to make mistakes. Unfortunately, unless you just stay in bed all day, mistakes happen. Even if you practice hard and do your best, you won't always make the basket or score the goal. No matter how much you study, you won't always get perfect grades. But you know what? Mistakes don't mean we're terrible or stupid; they mean we're human. We can learn from every single mistake we make and use that knowledge to improve. Keep that in mind as you pursue hand lettering and everything else you do. You are going to mess up; I guarantee it. Will you give up, or will you keep on trying, learning from what you did wrong and making next time better?

It's time to learn another lettering style you can use to add variety to your designs. We're going to take something you already know how to do and create a variation that looks like an entirely different font. Remember the Faux Calligraphy Print we learned in Chapter 5 (page 34)? This new alphabet is built on that foundation, but has a fun twist that makes it perfect to use for all kinds of festive occasions. This Polka Dot-Filled Alphabet is a great font to use on cards and envelopes, gift tags and more. Plus, you can make it unique every time you write by using different colors and even other patterns.

As we move into learning a new font, remember not to pressure yourself to letter perfectly every time. Just enjoy practicing and filling your book with art.

POLKA DOT-FILLED ALPHABET

The first two steps of this new alphabet are going to be exactly the same as what you do for the Faux Calligraphy Print (page 34), so you should be able to do them in no time.

STEP 1

Print your word.

We are going to practice with the word *trying*.

TRYING

STEP 2

Draw a double line wherever you have a downstroke.

If you forget where the downstrokes are, you can refer back to Chapter 5 (page 37) and look at the sample alphabet there, or look at the sample alphabet at the end of this chapter.

Here's where things start getting different.

STEP 3

Instead of coloring in the space between the double lines with black as we normally do, leave it blank or use another color.

STEP 4

Add polka dots in the spaces.

Lightly pressing the tip of a marker to the surface of your paper should create nice round, little dots. If you are trying to draw them over a dark color, you may want to use a white or light-colored gel pen (the gel will sit on top of the ink and make it a little easier to see).

That's all there is to it! Now you have a fun, playful print font that looks totally different from our Faux Calligraphy Print (page 34). Here's a look at the whole alphabet written in this style.

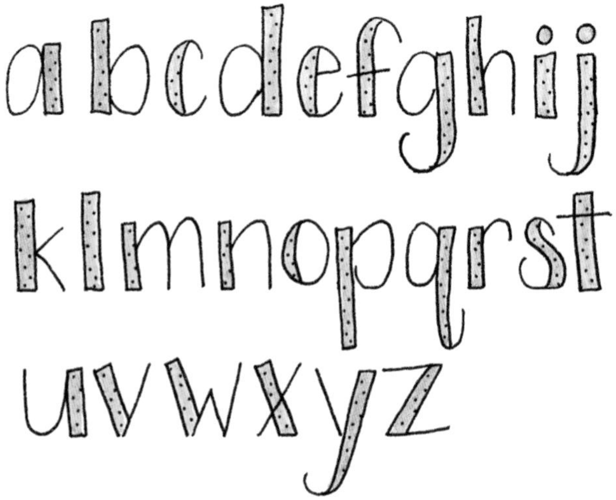

ABCDEFGHIJKL
MNOPQRSTUVW
XYZ

abcdefghij
klmnopqrst
uvwxyz

You can change the look of this font by using a pattern different from the polka dots such as stripes, hearts and zigzags. Here are a few words written in different patterns so you can refer to them as you create your designs.

FUN Love JOY

After you practice forming these letters in the space below, go ahead and create your masterpiece on the border page. First use a pencil and straightedge to draw horizontal lines so your words will be in a straight line. Write in your words, doing your best to keep them centered. I used a mix of our new Polka Dot–Filled Alphabet, Faux Calligraphy Print (page 34) and Funky Print Font (page 22). Draw two swirls (page 18) on the sides of the short "You Are" to add a little extra pizzazz to the design. Go over the pencil with your markers and then erase any pencil lines you can see. Since my Pattern Fill letters were purple, I used a white gel pen for the polka dots, so they really stand out. Feel free to use my sample quote as a guide for your own or create one in any way you like.

PRACTICE BELOW

EIGHT

DRAWING FESTIVE BANNERS

At the middle school I attended, the principal used to end morning announcements by saying, "Make it a great day—or not. The choice is yours!" There were definitely some days I didn't want to admit it, but he was right. We never know what a day is going to hold. Your birthday could turn out to be a rainy day, and someone could drop your cake on the floor. Or you might wake up one Monday to find out that school is cancelled because of snow, so you get to stay home and play all day! We don't get to decide all of the things that happen to us, but we do get to decide how we react to them. We can be optimistic and look on the bright side, even when something rotten happens, or we can be pessimistic and grumpy when things don't go our way. I don't know about you, but I'm a huge fan of Kid President, and I love the way he puts it: "I am a party! Everywhere I go is a party!" Now there's a kid who knows how to enjoy life! Instead of waiting for good things to happen, it's up to you and me to find our own fun. It's our choice to find ways to enjoy our day and be the party—or not. I'd much rather treat every day like a celebration than complain about all the things that went wrong. What about you? What can you celebrate today?

The set of doodles we're going to learn in this chapter are perfect for birthdays and all kinds of other celebrations. First we'll take a look at how to draw a basic banner. Then we'll try a different banner style with variations, so you have plenty to choose from when you want to make your art look extra festive. All of the fonts you've practiced so far will work with these doodles: Polka Dot-Filled Alphabet (page 46), Funky Print Font (page 22), Faux Calligraphy Script (page 11) and Faux Calligraphy Print (page 34). It's especially fun to letter inside the banners; you're going to love it. Then you can use the fonts and doodles together to create hand lettered cards, signs, wrapping paper, gifts and more! What are we waiting for? Let's get this party started!

BASIC BANNER
STEP 1

Draw a curving line.

Leave some space below it, then draw a second curving line underneath. This will be the top and bottom of your banner, so make sure you leave enough space to write in between the lines.

STEP 2

Connect the top and bottom of your banner with short vertical lines on both sides.

I like to make mine curve just a little bit to look more natural.

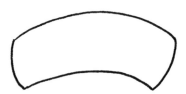

STEP 3

Draw a line about halfway up each side of your banner to create the tops of the tails.

The lines should curve upward a little bit.

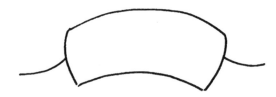

STEP 4

Finish off your tails.

To do this, draw a sideways *v*, then connect it to the bottom line of your banner. Don't worry about getting the sides totally even or exactly the same. That's the great thing about hand-drawn art: nothing has to be perfect!

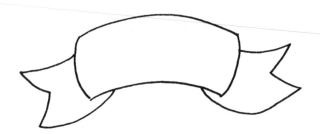

STEP 5

Make a small curving line connecting the bottom corner of your banner to the place where the tail connects to it.

This is what makes it look like the banner is folded and three-dimensional.

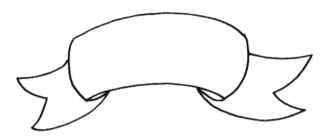

STEP 6

Add details if you'd like!

Some details I often add include coloring in the fold spaces and drawing accent lines on the top and on the tails. This part is totally optional. Have fun playing around with different accents to see what you like best!

Once your banner is finished, you're ready to write inside of it. I often use my banners for words like *happy birthday*, *celebrate* or *party time*. Make sure you pencil in your words first, though, so you don't run out of space. More than once, I've been writing with just a marker and ended up with *happy birt*.

The pennant banner is another banner style that's just as fun, but gives a totally different effect. While you can write in this kind too, it can also be used all by itself as a border or decoration for your designs. Take a look!

PENNANT BANNER

STEP 1

Draw a curving line.

This time, it's going to curve in the opposite direction, like a smile. The line will be the string that holds all your pennants together, so it can be as long or short as you want.

STEP 2

Draw a series of *v*'s along your line.

I like to start by making my first *v* in the center and then working my way out to each end. Try to keep all the *v*'s about the same size. As the line starts to curve, make sure to turn your paper while you're drawing so your pennants look realistic.

STEP 3

Color or write in your pennants.

Use any combination or pattern of colors you'd like for your pennants. In addition to coloring the pennants, I often add little highlights with a white gel pen. I like to color first, using the watercolor technique from Chapter 6 (page 40), and then write on top of the pennants once they are dry. To write in this kind of banner, you'll be able to put only one letter in each pennant. Count the letters in your word ahead of time to make sure you draw the right number of pennants.

Once you get comfortable with this kind of banner, you can experiment with shapes other than just the *v*. Instead of triangle pennants, try drawing rectangles with an upside-down *v* on the bottom. It's the same doodle, but with a twist. What other shapes can you think of that would be fun?

Use the space below to practice drawing, coloring and writing in banners. Then when you're ready, use the special border page to create the design inspired by the Kid President quote. Don't forget to color in the border too! To create the design the way I did, you'll want to start by drawing the basic banner, then writing the word *PARTY* inside in the Polka Dot–Filled Alphabet (page 46). Remember, it's a good idea to sketch with a pencil first, then go back over it with a marker later. This way you'll make sure everything fits and you like the spacing before you make it permanent. Above the banner, use your Funky Print Font (page 22) to write *I go is a*, following the same curve as the top of the banner. Then write *everywhere* above that in Faux Calligraphy Script (page 11). Color in your banner and letters using whatever colors you like, then add some simple swirls (page 18) above and below the banner to embellish your design. To color my banner, I used the watercolor technique we learned in Chapter 6 (page 40).

PRACTICE BELOW

NINE

THREE FLOWER DOODLES

Have you ever looked outside on a wet day and thought *rain, rain, go away*? Rain can mess up all kinds of plans and make a day feel just plain yucky. It can cancel sports games or practices, make us feel soggy at the bus stop and keep us from outdoor activities. But if we go without it long enough, we won't have flowers or grass or leaves on the trees. As annoying as it can be, rain is a necessary part of the cycle that keeps everything alive and beautiful. It's kind of like some of the situations in our lives. At the time, some of the things that happen to us feel pretty lousy. We might wish them away, but the truth is, they make us grow. Just as flowers can't bloom without rain, we can't grow without experiencing difficulties. If life were always easy and sunny, we'd never learn to be strong. Next time something happens that isn't especially great, ask yourself what you can learn from it. How can you use that situation to become wiser and stronger?

Some of my favorite ways to embellish lettered designs are with objects found in nature. Flowers in particular can really add a lot to a quote, and there's no end to how many different types of floral embellishments you can draw. Just like there are thousands of different plants and flowers in nature, there are thousands of ways to doodle them. In this chapter we are going to focus on three specific kinds of flowers, and then learn to combine them into pretty arrangements that will add a colorful touch to your artwork.

Let's take some time to learn to sketch those beautiful rain-watered flowers as we remember that the hard things in life can help us bloom.

SIMPLE ROUND FLOWER

Can everyone draw a messy circle? I thought so! That's all you need to create the first flower we'll be drawing in this chapter. Grab your markers and get ready to be amazed.

STEP 1

Draw a messy circle, tracing over it several times.

You'll want to make sure the marker you use for this drawing is either permanent or not water based. Otherwise, when you go back to color inside your lines, the marker could bleed.

STEP 2

Draw a bunch of dots in the center.

STEP 3

Color in your circle.

You can use any supplies or techniques you like to color in the flower. I love using the watercolor technique we learned in Chapter 6 (page 40), but you can also use any markers, crayons or colored pencils you happen to have on hand.

Now, let's try a little rose.

SPIRAL ROSE

STEP 1

Draw a small spiral, closing it off so that the end of the line touches the rest of the spiral.

Ta-da! You just made a tiny rosebud!

STEP 2

Color in your spiral.

I like to use the watercolor technique from Chapter 6 (page 40), but you can use any techniques and supplies you like.

The last flower we're going to learn has three petals and is seen from the side, so you won't be drawing its center.

EASY DAISY

STEP 1

Draw three petals, each beginning and ending in the same spot like a teardrop.
Draw the center petal a little taller than the others. You can also do this with five petals to make a bigger flower.

STEP 2

Draw several lines from the bottom of each petal up into the center.

STEP 3

Color your flower any way you like.
I like to add darker color or lines toward the bottom and get lighter as I go toward the top of the petals.

To create a floral arrangement, all we're going to do is sketch a mixture of these three flower types. I like to start with an odd number of the large messy-circle flowers, usually three. Sketch them in a little group with the center flower a little higher than the other two.

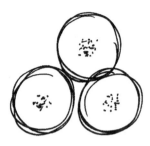

Next, add a few spiral roses to the mix.

Finally, add some daisies.

Fill in the extra space with leaves. To create a leaf, I draw a shape that has rounded sides and a point at each end. You can make your leaves as long, thin, wide or narrow as you want them to be. I like to use a variety of shapes and sizes since that's what you'd find in nature. For extra detail and realism, I add lines down the center of the leaves and sometimes shorter lines coming off of those to represent the veins.

That's all there is to it! Color them in however you like, and you have a beautiful arrangement of colorful flowers that will look pretty with anything you decide to letter. Each type of flower can also be used on its own. There's no wrong way to use a flower.

Use the space below to practice sketching and coloring your own flowers, and then go ahead and create the quote design on the border page. You'll want to start by drawing horizontal lines with a pencil to help you keep your quote straight, and then sketch the positions of your words with Faux Calligraphy Script (page 11). Next, pencil in your flowers where you want them to go, and then finish up by going over everything with a marker. Add simple swirls (page 18) along the sides for some extra embellishment. I recommend using the watercolor technique (page 40) to fill in your flowers because it will give you a smooth and blended look, but you can use any supplies you like. I have a feeling that once you're finished, you might want to draw some of these flowers on your notebooks and book covers too!

PRACTICE BELOW

TEN

FLORAL LETTERS

Like it or not, we all have good days, bad days and meh days. It's only natural that when things are going our way, we're in a great mood, whereas a bad day can put us in a funk. Our circumstances can definitely affect our attitudes. But true happiness doesn't depend on what's happening around us. Real joy can only come from the inside. Even on a bad day, we can find happiness in our friendships and families, and gratitude for all the things that we have. We can focus on the good instead of whatever has us feeling down. It's up to us whether we're going to complain or smile. When we start choosing joy, we'll find that even the tough days are easier to handle. Will you choose to let happiness bloom from your heart today?

Now that you've mastered a few flowers to add to your artwork, let's take them one step further. In this chapter we're going to look at how to make the flowers part of your letters themselves. While you could certainly do this to every letter you write, it's usually better to stick to the first letter of each word. Too much of this embellishment can make your artwork feel busy or hard to read. This is a fun way to decorate someone's name on the front of an envelope or on a name tag.

As we work on lettering this quote with flowers, let it remind you not to allow a tough circumstance to steal your joy. Let's get to it!

FLORAL LETTERS

The floral letter skills we're going to look at in this chapter will actually work with just about any style of alphabet you like best. We will be practicing with the Faux Calligraphy Print (page 34), but you can also do this same thing to Faux Calligraphy Script (page 11), your Funky Print Font (page 22) or any of the other lettering styles. The basic idea is that we're going to create a little vine wrapping around one side of our letter, and then put some pretty blooms on it. Here's how:

STEP 1

Write your letter.

We are going to start with a capital *L* in our Faux Calligraphy Print (page 34). You can fill in the space with color like I did if you want.

STEP 2

Draw a wavy line around the thick part of the letter.

This will be your vine. You can keep it simple, or you can really try to make it look like it's wrapping around. I like to use a fine-tip green marker for this step. I try to make mine look as realistic as possible, so I think about where the vine would be going behind the letter and make sure not to draw over the letter in those spots.

STEP 3

Add a few flowers to your vine.

Remember, odd numbers of things always look better, so you may want to draw three or five blooms. I used the little spiral roses we learned in Chapter 9 (page 62).

STEP 4

Add leaves.

Draw a little leaf anywhere you have a bit of extra space on your vine to fill it up. Leave a little space in between some of the leaves, though, so it doesn't look too busy.

It's that simple—now you have a pretty flowered letter. This is a great way to monogram something, don't you think? Now that you've learned the basic technique, you can experiment by using different kinds of flowers too. Here's how it looks when you use the other two types we learned in Chapter 9 (page 60).

When you're using the Faux Calligraphy Script (page 11), a good rule to follow is to put your vine around the thick downstroke part of the letter. If there's more than one, stick with one of the letter's sides. For other font styles, I usually just keep my vines on the left side of the letter. In order to keep my designs from looking too busy, I add flowers to the first letter of each word rather than every single letter.

Take some time to practice in the space below. Try using a variety of letters, starting with your initials. Then sketch our happiness quote on the border page. Remember to pencil in the words first, and then go back over them with a marker. Add flowers and vines to some of the letters to decorate the quote. Add a simple flower arrangement from Chapter 9 (page 60) on the bottom and simple swirls (page 18) on the sides. You can use my sample as a guide, or you can recreate the quote in your own way.

PRACTICE BELOW

ELEVEN

ANIMAL DOODLES

Whether we're cat lovers, dog people or crazy about guinea pigs, pets hold a special place in our hearts. Sometimes it feels like they understand us better than people do! Pets really become a part of the family, and they can actually help us be less stressed. It might sound crazy, but studies have even concluded that pet owners live longer because of the physical and psychological effects our furry friends have on us. You might want to curl up next to your favorite pet as we head into this chapter, because it's all about animals!

What could be more fun for embellishing your art than animal doodles? While they're not a perfect fit for every quote you want to letter, they're great accents for envelopes, cards and lots of other projects. Draw them on the cover of your notebook or use them to create a sign for your room. Drawing animals can seem intimidating, but they're really just made of simple shapes put together in a certain way. Once you learn the basics, you'll be able to figure out how to draw just about any animal you want! We'll look at a few examples and then combine one with our lettering to illustrate a quote for all the pet lovers out there.

DRAWING ANIMALS

There are so many ways to draw animals, and so many different animals to draw, that there's no way we could possibly cover them all in one chapter. To keep things simple, we are going to focus on animal faces, but you can try adding bodies too!

STEP 1

Draw a circle.

This will be the animal's face. Use an oval shape for a cat.

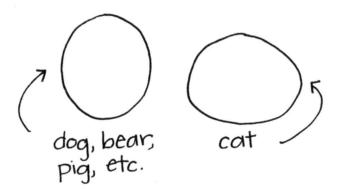

dog, bear, pig, etc.

cat

STEP 2

Draw semicircles or triangles for ears.

Bear ears are rounded, while cat ears are more pointed. Depending on the breed of dog, there are a variety of shapes you can use like triangles for a chihuahua or long ovals for a beagle.

bear   cat   bunny

Pig   dog   dog

STEP 3

Add a nose.

Depending on your animal, this might be a circle, an oval or an upside-down triangle. If you like, you could even use a heart shape.

STEP 4

Draw two eyes.

These can simply be colored-in circles, or you can be more detailed. For a cat, you'll want to make an outer shape that's pointed on both ends like a football, and then draw circles inside.

STEP 5

Add a mouth.

The easiest way to do this is by drawing a little smile. If your animal is a cat or a dog, you may want to draw a line coming straight down from the nose too.

Sketch any details that are unique to your animal.

For a panda, you'll draw an oval around each eye. Cats will get whiskers. Many types of animals have a circle around the nose and mouth area.

That's all there is to it! These basic steps are the building blocks you need to draw whatever animals you like best. One fun way to embellish animal quotes and illustrations is with little paw prints like the ones I used in the sample design. All you have to do to create those is draw a shape that looks like a triangle with rounded edges, and then draw three or four little ovals over it—easy peasy!

A fun project idea is to turn this design into a bookmark by cutting a piece of cardstock and doing your lettering on it. Punch a hole in the top and add a ribbon or string if you like, or leave it as is. It makes a great gift for teachers and friends!

Use the practice area to create all kinds of different animals. Then use your favorite to illustrate the quote on your border page. As always, you'll want to start by lightly sketching your guidelines in pencil to keep your lettering straight. To create this design, you'll be combining Funky Print Font (page 22), Faux Calligraphy Script (page 11) and Polka Dot-Filled Alphabet (page 46). Write the words *road* and *my heart* in color to make them stand out, and use color to fill in the Polka Dot-Filled Alphabet. Now you've emphasized the most important parts of the saying. Once your quote is written, it's time to embellish it! I added two simple swirls (page 18), one on each side of the design, and a little paw print above each one. Finally, I drew a cat at the bottom and colored it using the watercolor technique (page 40). You can use whatever colors you like and your own favorite animal to make your design personal and unique!

PRACTICE BELOW

COMIC BOOK PRINT

Cupcakes ARE JUST muffins THAT BELIEVED IN miracles !

Do you believe anything could happen? I hope so, because the world needs more people who do. When you believe anything is possible, that's when you're able to do impossible things. Imagine if Alexander Graham Bell hadn't believed it was possible for people to communicate from one home to another. We'd have no such thing as the telephone, let alone the smartphones we do everything on today. If Karl Benz hadn't believed an engine could power a vehicle, we'd still be traveling in horse-drawn carriages. Thank goodness for the dreamers, the visionaries, the people who believe that anything can be. Will we ever be able to travel through time? Will cars fly? Who knows? When I was in elementary school, there were people who thought we would never be able to see a person when we talked to them on the phone. FaceTime, anyone? It's up to you to be someone who keeps believing in things you can't yet see, so you can help change the world.

One way to make the world a better place is by creating beautiful things, just like you're doing now, especially if you use your talents to brighten someone's day. This funny quote is all about cupcakes. Do you know a cupcake lover in your life who would enjoy getting a card with your new skills? Let's work on lettering this quote with the help of a new font and, of course, a cupcake doodle.

Everyone loves to laugh! That's why we tell jokes and share memes, and why comic books became a popular form of art. Have you ever noticed that the fonts used in comics tend to have their own unique style? Most of the writing in a comic book, aside from the big sound effects like "ka-pow," is small and written in all capital letters that are easy to read. The idea is that the words still look artistic, but they don't take away from the main images of the characters and action. In this chapter we're going to take a look at how to write in that comic book style, so we can use it in a similar way. It's the perfect font to use for those little words and phrases like *and* or *in the* that are part of a quote, but not the main focus.

COMIC BOOK PRINT

Remember, one of the most important things about the print in comic books is that it's simple and plain. There aren't a bunch of fancy embellishments to the style itself. Instead, it's designed to be a hand-drawn way to communicate words without taking away from the rest of the artwork. In this chapter's quote, the cupcake doodle is our main focus, as well as the words *cupcake*, *muffin* and *miracles*. Those words will be written in one of our more eye-catching fonts, and then we'll write the connecting words in Comic Book Print.

There are two other things to keep in mind about this style. First, comic book lettering is almost always written in all capital letters. Second, the letters have a handwritten look to them, so don't focus on trying to make your Comic Book Print look perfect. Comic book letters are usually slightly slanted to the right. I like to use a brush pen for this writing style because it gives a more uneven, hand-drawn look, so if you have one, you'll want to grab that for this chapter. If not, any fine-tip marker will do.

COMICS ARE FUN

To emphasize a word in this font, you'll want to make the letters darker and write them on more of a slant than your other words. If you are using a brush pen, you can make them darker by pressing harder while you write. If not, simply retrace the letters to make them a little bit thicker.

VERY VERY VERY

Here is a sample alphabet showing how you can form each letter.

ABCDEFGHIJKLMNOP
QRSTUVWXYZ %.$/|\

Spend some time practicing individual letters and then putting together some short words in the space below.

PRACTICE BELOW

Now, it's time to work on our cupcake quote! Here's how to illustrate your cupcake.

STEP 1

Draw a shape that's similar to a leaf but open at the bottom.

You can trace mine a few times to help you figure out how it works. This shape will be the tip of the frosting on your cupcake.

STEP 2

Under your shape, draw a set of parentheses.

The top of each curving line should touch the side of your first shape, and they should come out a little bit wider too. This makes the second layer of your frosting.

STEP 3

Draw another set of parentheses under the first set, again coming out a little wider than the layer above. Then connect them with a curving horizontal line.

This will be the bottom of the frosting. The top part of the cupcake is now complete. This is also how to draw a poo emoji, just color it brown and add eyes and a smile. But you didn't hear that from me.

STEP 4

Draw two vertical lines below your cupcake top.

These should start out wider at the top, and then get closer together.

STEP 5

Connect your lines with a curving horizontal line to finish the cupcake bottom.

After connecting the lines, draw vertical lines to add detail to the cupcake liner.

STEP 6

Add color using the watercolor technique from Chapter 6 (page 40) or any other supplies you choose.

You can add some extra details too, like sprinkles and a cherry on top. I even gave my cherry a little highlight line with a white gel pen. Feel free to be as creative and colorful as you'd like when decorating your cupcake.

Once you've practiced your Comic Book Print and a few cute cupcakes, it's time to work on your quote design. Start by using a pencil to sketch a few horizontal guidelines, and then use a mixture of Comic Book Print and Faux Calligraphy Script (page 11) or Polka Dot–Filled Alphabet (page 46) to write the words. Finish it off with a colorful cupcake, and you'll have a masterpiece!

PRACTICE BELOW

THIRTEEN

COMIC DOODLES

There is definitely something to be said for keeping things clean, neat and organized. People who do can always find what they need and don't have to spend half an hour looking for their left shoe. (Not that I've ever done that . . . ahem.) Did you know, though, that most creative people are more inclined to be messy? It's how our brains work. We think abstractly and get lost in our ideas, rather than focus on the details in front of us. And you know what? That's okay! After a good day of making projects, I usually have paint on my face, my hands, in my hair and, sometimes, even on the cat. Artists are allowed to make messes; just look at Jackson Pollock and his splatter paintings! If he weren't willing to get messy, we'd never have any of those masterpieces. Roll up your sleeves and create something, even if it means you make a mess too. Express yourself and don't feel bad if you're never as organized as some of your friends. Your brain is doing its own thing, Picasso!

Now that we've learned to print like a comic book artist, let's have some fun with a few comic-inspired doodles. Quote bubbles and comic borders can be great frames for a hand lettered phrase, especially if it happens to be a funny one. Whether you draw a character who's speaking the words or not, these doodles make any quote feel like it's right off the pages of a comic book.

There are several types of these word embellishments found in comic books, all of which work really well with hand lettered art. In this chapter we're going to look at three—the standard quote bubble, the thought bubble and the ka-pow bubble.

QUOTE BUBBLE

The quote bubble is what you normally see when a character is speaking. It's basically an oval or a rectangle with a little triangle shape coming off of the bottom that points to the character's mouth.

Here are a couple of examples. To create them, all you do is sketch your shape and draw the *v* of the triangle on the bottom. You can do this all in one step, or you can start by drawing the shapes separately in pencil, and then tracing the outline with a marker.

THOUGHT BUBBLE

The thought bubble is used when a character is just thinking something without necessarily saying it aloud. This one looks more like a cloud, and instead of having the *v*-shape at the bottom, it floats above the character's head along with a few other little circles or clouds. All you have to do is draw a series of bumps in a basic oval or rectangle and add small circles leading down to the character's head.

KA–POW BUBBLE

The ka-pow bubble is my favorite. I call it that because it's the shape you usually see when there's a big, loud sound effect in a cartoon. It has lots of pointy lines and makes a big impact. To draw it, I like to make a series of *v* shapes, alternating the heights so they're small, large, small, large and so on.

When you use these kinds of doodles with your lettering, you'll want to pencil your words inside the doodle to make sure you have the spacing right. Just as with the banners, it's easy to run out of room, so you don't want to just start writing in marker without planning first, or you may have to start all over again. Another option is to write your phrase first, then draw the comic bubble around it. That way you'll be sure all your words fit inside.

Comic Book Print (page 81) looks perfect with these doodles, but any of the other font styles will work really well too. Feel free to mix and match until the quote looks just the way you want it. There's practice space on the next page to get you started. See which doodles are your favorites, and then choose one to use in the lettered quote design.

To create the sample, I wrote my quote in a mixture of Comic Book Print (page 81) and Funky Print Font (page 22). You'll notice that this time it's not perfectly horizontal, so when you sketch your guidelines in pencil, you'll want to do it on a slight angle. After the quote is lettered, draw your favorite type of bubble around it. I used an orange marker to trace over my ka-pow bubble, and then I added some extra pop by taking a yellow marker and drawing some accent lines around the bubble. As always, you can use any colors and styles you like to make the design your own.

PRACTICE BELOW

EXPRESS YOURSELF: A HAND LETTERING WORKBOOK FOR KIDS!

FOURTEEN

DESCENDER LETTER FLOURISHES

One of the best things about being young is that you have unlimited opportunities ahead of you. Can I just tell you this one thing? Don't give up on your dreams. Chase them. Pursue them. Find ways to make them real. The happiest people I know are the ones who are doing what they love. Following a dream takes a lot of dedication and hard work, and sometimes it ends up looking a little different than you thought. Not everyone will end up becoming a professional athlete or a movie star, but there are still ways to follow even those passions. You can play on a recreational sports team, be a coach or become an announcer. You can perform in, direct or choreograph community theater productions. You can form your own band or sing with a local group. There are all kinds of ways to pursue the things you care about most and make them a part of your future. Don't give up on your dreams just because you think they're impossible or because someone says so. Chase after them and you might be surprised at what you catch!

Let's learn how to letter ourselves a reminder to hold on to our dreams.

Remember when we first learned about basic flourishes all the way back in Chapter 2 (page 17)? By now, you're practically a pro at using those to decorate your designs. It's time to take things to the next level by learning how to add flourishes to your letters themselves. There are certain letters, especially the ones with ascenders and descenders, that are perfect for adding a little extra flair. We're going to try out a few different ways to embellish those letters that are much easier than they look.

DESCENDER LETTER FLOURISHES

We're going to begin adding a little extra pizzazz to our letters by focusing on letters with descenders. Remember, descenders are lines that extend down past the main body of the letter, as in the letters *y, g* and *j*. There are more ways to embellish these letters than we can count, so there's no way to cover them all. Instead, we're going to look at five of the most popular ones and work on mastering those. You can use these flourishes wherever the letter appears, whether it's at the beginning, middle or end of a word. I'll show you how to embellish your ascender letters in Chapter 15 (page 103).

SIMPLE SWIRL

The simple swirl is the easiest flourish to do. Write your letter as you always do, and then just add a little swirl onto the end of your line that crosses back over the descender before you pick up your pen. See? Easy peasy.

LOOPING TAIL

A looping tail flourish is just what it sounds like. Write your letter normally, and then add a little downward loop to the end of the tail, just like the loops you make in your basic flourishes. Make sure the loop points down because otherwise it can resemble a tiny *e* and make your word hard to read. You'll also want to keep it small so it's obviously just a little decoration and no one mistakes it for an *o*.

LOOP-DE-LOO

I like to call this next variation the loop-de-loo because then it sounds as fun as it looks! You'll start making your letter as usual, and then after you bring your pen back up, make a small downward loop before you cross over the descender line. You can see in the samples that you can play around with how large to make the loop and where you position it.

BACKTRACK

Backtrack flourishes are a little different from the others because they go out to the left of your letter. This can be a neat effect if you use it at the end of a word because it's a fancy way to underline something. To do this, you'll start like the loop-de-loo, but then, instead of finishing your tail up and to the right, you'll go to the left and end with a little swirl. Take a look.

CROSSOVER LOOP

The last flourish we're going to look at is the hardest, but I think it's the coolest-looking one. I call it the crossover loop. It starts like the loop-de-loo and the backtrack, but this time, after making the loop, you're going to go a little to the left, and then back to the right, crossing your line through the loop you just drew.

What do you think? Aren't these fun? Take some time in the practice space or on another sheet of paper to try these five different styles and experiment with a few of the other letters like *j* and *g*. Then try writing some simple words like *joy* and *you* using flourishes on your descender letters. In my example below, the *j* has a crossover loop, the first *y* has a simple swirl and the second *y* has a loop-de-loo. Have fun with your embellishments!

Our quote features three letters we can embellish: two *y*'s and a *g*. Sketch out the words in pencil to properly space them on the page and play around with the different kinds of flourishes to see which ones you want to use in your finished design. I alternated using simple Faux Calligraphy Script (page 11) and Funky Print Font (page 22).

Since the theme of the quote is dreams, clouds and stars are a great way to illustrate the design. To create stars like mine, use a pencil to draw some basic five-pointed stars, then erase the lines going through the center. Color them in with a marker or the watercolor technique (page 40), and then erase the rest of the pencil outline. Clouds are just a series of bumps and swirls; there's no wrong way to draw them! Use my examples as a guide and try sketching a few in pencil. Then when you get the hang of it, trace over the ones you like with a marker. You can also add a simple crescent-shaped moon. Feel free to copy my sample design or try your own combination of fonts and embellishments.

PRACTICE BELOW

FIFTEEN

ASCENDER FLOURISHES & CROSSING YOUR *TS*

Wouldn't it be nice if we lived in a world where doing the right thing was always easy? Unfortunately, sometimes, it's just the opposite. I'm sure you don't have to think too hard to remember a time when it would have been more convenient to tell a little white lie. What if a cashier gave you the wrong change and handed you a ten-dollar bill instead of one dollar? It would be easier to keep it than to give the extra money back. Doing what we know is right can even be an unpopular choice, like if a friend wants you to lie so they don't get in trouble with their parents. The bottom line, though, is that no matter how hard it is, the right thing is always the right thing. Choosing to be honest might lead to consequences you don't enjoy, but in the long run, people will see that you're someone who can be trusted. Your friends, parents and teachers will know they can believe what you say, and that will end up being much better than escaping trouble in the moment. Plus, you never have to feel guilty when you do the right thing! It's always the best choice.

Speaking of choices, we're going to look at some choices in this chapter for embellishing individual letters in your projects. Let's jump in!

In the last chapter, we learned five different ways to add a little extra flair to letters that descend past our baseline. But those aren't the only letters that are perfect for embellishing. We can also have some fun with ascender letters, and don't forget about crossing our *t*'s! In this chapter we're going to learn how to take letters like *b*, *d* and *t* to the next level with some more flourishes that look a lot harder to create than they actually are.

ASCENDER LETTER FLOURISHES

It's time to learn a few more letter flourishes that will give our artwork a real wow factor! As you try these, a good trick is to keep your pen moving pretty quickly so that your lines will look smooth. If you're thinking hard and moving your pen slowly to get everything just right, you'll find that you end up with shaky lines and you won't like the end result nearly as much. Remember, we're just practicing and learning, so if you make a mistake, all you have to do is try again.

Now, let's talk about the letters we're going to embellish in this chapter. Do you remember what an ascender is? It's a line on a letter that extends above the letter's main body. Just like a descender, it can be made extra fancy by adding a little flourish. The most common way to do this is by starting a line to the left of where you want the letter to go, as in the examples.

You can also embellish a little more by starting that line with a little loop before continuing over to make your letter.

Now, we're going to apply some of these same embellishments to the line we make to cross our *t*. First, we're going to make that same line starting with a loop that we just used in the last step.

The main thing to keep in mind when you're embellishing a *t* is that the ends of your line should always go in opposite directions. If both ends curl down, your *t* will look like it's frowning. If both ends go up, it will look like a smile. Instead, what we want is a line that curves up on one end and down on the other. This will create visual balance in your design.

You can make the crossbar as long as you want. It can be even on both sides, or you can make it longer on one side than on the other.

Every now and then you might get a really fun word that allows you to cross your *t* using the line from another letter, like *thanks* or *trade*. The technical name for combining two letters to make a new shape is *ligature*.

There's no specific rule for when to use which type of embellishment; that's part of the joy of lettering. It's totally up to you how much, when and where you use these flourishes. Usually, I look at the words themselves and where the letters are positioned to help me decide how I want to write them. In the practice space, try these different flourishes and see which ones you like best. Start out by practicing letters, and then move on to simple words like *dad*, *hat* and *bat*. You can even combine these new skills with what we worked on in the last chapter (page 96) by writing *boy* or *dog*.

Our special quote for this chapter is written in Faux Calligraphy Script (page 11) and accented with a pennant banner (page 56). First sketch the words (don't forget your horizontal guidelines!) and experiment with what kind of embellishments you want to use on the letters. Then when you like your design, trace over it with your markers. I wanted to accent the words *right* and *easy*, so I traced those in bright colors while the rest of the quote is written in black. To finish the design, I drew a pennant banner (page 56) over the quote and used the watercolor technique (page 40) to color it in with the same pink and orange I used in my lettering. This ties the design together and makes it pleasing to the eye.

PRACTICE BELOW

BASIC BOUNCE LETTERING

What would you say if I told you one of my biggest heroes is only seventeen years old? She's not a famous movie star or athlete, but she has done more to change the world in the last five years than I have in my entire life. Mallory Fundora was just eleven when a children's choir from Uganda visited her school. As she talked with the kids and found out about the struggles their families face, she began to feel like she wanted to do something to make their lives better. That year for Christmas, she told her parents that all she wanted was to help the children in Africa. With some help from her mom, Mallory began a nonprofit organization called Project Yesu that provides food, clothing and education to kids in Uganda. Mallory matches individual children with sponsors who donate money for their schooling, and she also visits Uganda in person every summer to spend time with the families, physically meeting their needs and forming relationships with them.

It humbles me to think of all the lives Mallory has touched just because she was willing to be a difference-maker. She saw something in the world that she wanted to change, so she got busy changing it! Mallory didn't let the fact that she was "just a kid" stop her, and neither should you. There's no limit to what you can do if you put your mind to it. Whether you're ten or twelve or ninety-two, you can make a difference. What is the biggest change you wish to see in the world? How could you do something today to start making it happen, right where you are?

To learn more about Mallory's story, check out www.projectyesu.org.

Let's take some time now to create a design that will remind us not to just wish for change but to be difference-makers!

When we first learn to write, one of the things we're expected to do is keep our letters lined up straight along the baseline we talked about in Chapter 3 (page 22). But one of my favorite things about art is that sometimes you get to break the rules on purpose to create a more interesting design. Many artists live by the motto, "Learn the rules like a pro so you can break them like an artist." One of the most common ways hand lettering artists do this is by using a style called bounce lettering, where they choose not to have a straight baseline. Instead, the letters seem to bounce around inside the word at all different heights and positions. This gives your design a whimsical and free feeling, and it's nice for us as artists because we don't have to worry about keeping everything perfectly straight for once!

BOUNCE LETTERING

Are you ready to break the rules? We're going to use our Faux Calligraphy Script (page 11), but instead of drawing a horizontal baseline to guide us, we're going to use a wavy one instead! Take a look.

STEP 1

Take your pencil and begin drawing a wavy line across the page.

STEP 2

Using Faux Calligraphy Script (page 11), pencil the word *change* on the wavy baseline.

STEP 3

Trace over your word with a marker.

It's okay if your marker doesn't match up exactly with the pencil lines. Write quickly and confidently to get the smoothest lines using the penciled letters just as a basic guide.

All that's left to do is erase your pencil lines, and you have the word *change* written in bounce lettering!

Are you ready to try a new word? Let's write *world* using the same steps.

Eventually, you'll be able to vary the heights of your letters without actually drawing a baseline, but for starters, this is a good way to get the idea. There's no right or wrong way to do bounce lettering. The idea is that your letters don't have to be in any specific position. Don't worry about what goes where; it's totally up to you! In the practice space, try your hand at this technique. Focus on the words *change* and *world* since you'll be using them in the quote design on the border page, but you can also try writing your name and anything else you like using bounce lettering.

When you're ready to letter your design, start the same way by sketching the wavy lines and the positions of your words in pencil. You can change up the fonts for variety—I paired my bouncy Faux Calligraphy Script (page 11) with Funky Print Font (page 22). Once again, I used color for the words I wanted to emphasize and black for the rest. Sketch any embellishments you want to add too. Since the quote talks about the world, I created a globe by drawing a circle and a few wavy shapes to indicate the continents. Don't worry about being perfectly accurate. General shapes will be enough to show that it's the world, especially when you've colored it in with the watercolor technique (page 40).

I also drew a little stand for my globe using a half circle for the base and a line going around one side of the earth. To make a curving arrow like mine, just draw any style of curved or looping line you like, and then add a triangle to one end and a tail to the other. It's just like the basic arrow we learned in Chapter 6 (page 40), but with a curving line instead of a straight horizontal one. Once you've got your sketch just how you like it, you can go over everything in marker and erase the pencil lines when you're finished.

PRACTICE BELOW

SEVENTEEN

BASIC BRUSH TECHNIQUE

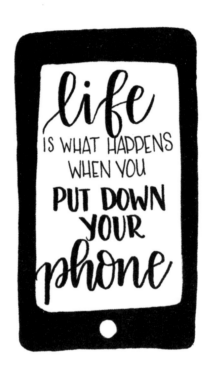

Have you ever been around someone who is with you, but not really paying attention? I've had plenty of experiences trying to tell a friend or a family member something important, but they didn't even hear me because they were focused on their phones. It's super frustrating, isn't it? But I have to admit there are times I'm guilty of doing the exact same thing. This summer, I was at a baseball game and I missed seeing a home run because I was posting on Instagram. I'm not gonna lie; it's really easy to get sucked into the digital world. Playing games, posting on social media and texting with friends is fun! But there comes a time when we need to put down our devices and appreciate what's going on right in front of us. Be aware of how much of your attention is on a device. Then challenge yourself to put it down and be in the moment. You might be surprised at all you've been missing!

Ever since the first chapter in this book, we've been creating a brush lettered look using our Faux Calligraphy Script (page 11). It works really well and it's easy to do. However, there's another way to get the same look using a special tool, a brush pen. It's an art technique that requires a good bit of practice and repetition before you get the hang of it, but once you do, it will get in your muscle memory, just like riding a bike. The trick is to control how wide your lines are by changing the amount of pressure you apply to the pen while you're writing. In this chapter I want to introduce you to the basics of this technique so that you can practice it and decide if it's something you want to work on mastering. Before you start, make sure you have the right type of pen, like the Tombow Fudenosuke, the Tombow Dual Brush Pen or something else specifically labeled *brush pen* or this won't work. You can easily find brush pens online or in your local craft and hobby store.

BRUSH TECHNIQUE

Before we begin talking about how to use the brush pen, take a minute to look at the pen's tip. If you are using a Tombow Dual Brush Pen, make sure you're looking at the brush side that's under the colored cap, rather than the bullet tip. Press the tip onto a piece of paper and watch what happens. It bends! Unlike a regular bullet-tip marker, a brush tip is flexible and is meant to act like a paintbrush. Let's look at what that means for our lettering.

STEP 1

Press down on your marker and draw a vertical line coming toward yourself.

Look how thick and dark that line is. That's because of the pressure you applied. Try that a few more times to get the hang of how that feels. Don't be afraid to press a little bit hard; the pen was made to do this exact thing.

STEP 2

Without applying a lot of pressure, lightly move the pen upward on your paper, away from yourself.

These lines should be lighter and thinner than the set you just drew in Step 1.

STEP 3

Alternate your lines so you have a pattern of thick, thin, thick, thin and so on.

The brush tip responds to the amount of pressure you use. Practice using light pressure as you draw upward and harder pressure as you draw downward. This is how you can get that mixture of thick and thin lines as you write a word. The key is to develop consistency.

Are you ready to try turning these lines into some letters? The most important thing to remember is that, just like in our Faux Calligraphy Script (page 11), downstrokes are thick and upstrokes and horizontal lines are thin. That means whenever you're writing a line and the pen is moving down on the page, you should be pressing hard. Anytime your pen is moving away from you, you need to release the pressure and hold the pen lightly. If you keep that in mind, you're on your way to mastering brush lettering.

STEP 4

Form a printed capital *T*. Start with a downstroke (don't forget to press!) and then a light horizontal stroke across the top.

Make a few *T*s in a row. The more you practice, the better your letters will start to look.

STEP 5

Now, let's write an *A*. You'll start with a thin diagonal upstroke, and then a thick downstroke and then a thin line across the middle.

Here are a few other letters that use only straight lines for you to practice your brush technique. These are the easiest ones to start with. Keep practicing! Then once you're feeling comfortable, you can move on to letters with loops and curves.

AEFHIKLMNTVW

When you write a letter with rounded sides, just start pressing harder when your pen starts to move downward and release the pressure when you start to move back up again. Using an o as an example, start at the top and press hard as you go down and to the left. Then as you go up to the right, lighten your grip for the thin line. It takes a little while to get the hang of this part, but practice definitely makes progress! Just keep trying and you'll get it.

ooooo

These sample alphabets will help you see where the downstrokes and upstrokes are in each letter. It's okay if you form your letters differently than I do, just pay attention to which parts of the letters are thick and thin. Take some time to practice this technique at your own pace. Don't get discouraged or expect to be a pro in just one day; this is a skill that takes a lot of repetition and hard work to master.

Aa Bb Cc Dd Ee Ff
Gg Hh Ii Jj Kk
Ll Mm Nn Oo
Pp Qq Rr Ss Tt Uu
Vv Ww Xx Yy Zz

Aa Bb Cc Dd Ee Ff Gg Hh
Ii Jj Kk Ll Mm Nn Oo
Pp Qq Rr Ss Tt Uu Vv
Ww Xx Yy Zz

This chapter's quote design is a combination of several of our fonts: Faux Calligraphy Script (page 11), Faux Calligraphy Print (page 34) and Funky Print Font (page 22). When you get to the parts that you'd typically write in Faux Calligraphy Script or Faux Calligraphy Print, try using this brush technique instead. You can practice in a sketchbook first to get the hang of it, and remember that we're not going for perfection. This is all about learning and trying new things, even when they're a little tricky. Start by sketching your pencil lines and creating your lettered quote. Then turn it into a phone by drawing two rectangles around it, one inside the other. You can trace an actual phone, use a ruler or freehand this part. Color the space in between the rectangles to create the edges of the phone. I drew a small circle at the bottom of mine to represent the home button on my iPhone.

PRACTICE BELOW

EIGHTEEN

AMPERSANDS

Life is full of things that can make us feel stressed out. School is a big one. You've got homework, classwork, tests and grades to worry about. You also have friendships and relationships with your parents and siblings, which are great, but obviously have conflicts sometimes. Then there's the big question everyone always asks, "What do you want to be when you grow up?" Those are just a few of the things that can make you feel anything but calm. When the stress starts to build up, what do you do to help yourself relax? One of the things that helps me the most is to create something. Even if what I make isn't amazing, the process of letting my creativity come out helps me to refocus and calm down. Believe it or not, doing the exercises in this book or practicing your lettering in a sketchbook can be a much-needed way to relieve stress. It's no accident that my first lettering book is titled *Hand Lettering for Relaxation*! As you practice your skills, let yourself forget about whatever problems you may be facing and just create for a while.

Let's take some time to relax as we look at another embellishment to add to your skill set.

One of the most common words we use in the English language is the conjunction *and*. Rather than spelling out the word, we often use a symbol in its place. Some people use a plus sign, whereas others use a symbol called the ampersand. Here's a quick history lesson about where it came from (don't worry, there won't be a test). In Latin, the word for *and* is "et." Back in the first century, people began writing the *e* and *t* together as one symbol in old Roman cursive. Remember in Chapter 15 (page 103) how we talked about something called a ligature, which is the combination of two letters to make one new shape? That's exactly what happened here. The *e* and *t* merged together to create the symbol we now call an ampersand and still use today twenty centuries later! In this chapter we're going to learn some artistic ways to draw an ampersand that we can use to embellish our hand lettered designs.

There are many ways to draw and embellish an ampersand. We're going to start by creating the basic shape, and then looking at some variations.

BASIC AMPERSAND
STEP 1
Draw a shape that resembles the left half of the number 8.

Add a tail.

That's all there is to it! See how it resembles a capital cursive *E* and a *t* combined?

LOOPING AMPERSAND

One simple way to make the ampersand look fancier is by adding three little loops: one at the top, one in the center and one right before the tail.

FAUX CALLIGRAPHY AMPERSAND

Another variation of the ampersand is to use our trusty Faux Calligraphy Script (page 11). Just draw double lines wherever you would move your pen downward, and then color in the space with either a black marker or a different color. You can also add a pattern, like our Polka Dot–Filled Alphabet (page 46).

MORE AMPERSAND INSPIRATION

Here are some other different styles of ampersands. Some are elegant, whereas others are more playful and fun. When you create a design, choose the one that fits best with your quote and the fonts you're using.

In the practice space below, you can experiment with these styles and even try creating some of your own. Then head over to the border page to create the quote design. You'll want to start by sketching your pencil guidelines, and then pencil in your words in a mixture of Faux Calligraphy Script (page 11) or Brush Lettering (page 116) and Funky Print Font (page 22). Be sure to draw your favorite ampersand as a focal point in the center of the design. I chose to embellish my quote with flowers (page 60) like the messy circle, the spiral rose and the easy daisy, but you can choose any of the other embellishments you've learned. When you're pleased with your sketch, add color with your markers and the watercolor technique (page 40), and then erase any pencil lines you can still see.

PRACTICE BELOW

NINETEEN

GALAXY EFFECT

I use the word *love* a lot. I say it to my family, but I also use it to describe my feelings for my cat, pizza, Netflix and plenty of other things too. Honestly, I think there should be another stronger word I could use when I'm talking about the people I love most, because even though I could eat pizza for three meals a day, it just doesn't compare. Did you know that in Greek, there are three words for love? My favorite is the word *agape* because it stands for love that is absolutely unconditional, unchanging and self-sacrificing. It's when you care about someone enough to give them something you really wanted for yourself. It's the kind of love that stands the test of time and distance and disagreements. When my best friend had a tragedy in her life, she called me at 3:00 a.m. and knew I would answer because of agape. When I was up against a deadline and couldn't do it all myself, she dropped everything to come and help me because of agape. The people in your life who put your needs ahead of their own are the people whose love is worth more than anything else in the world. Let them know how much it means to you to have their love in your life.

There's something magical about outer space. Maybe that's why we love all things galaxy-themed so much. Something about the vastness, the colors and the stars makes us want to recreate them in our art. Back in our watercolor chapter, Chapter 6 (page 40), we learned to paint and blend with Tombow Dual Brush Pens. In this chapter we're going to take those skills a step further by adding in our Basic Brush Lettering technique (page 116) to create galaxy effect lettering that's out of this world! The tip of the water pen is going to act just like our brush pen did and respond to the amount of pressure we apply when we write.

As we learn to letter this chapter's quote, you might want to think about using your art as a gift for one of those people! Remember, you can photograph or scan your artwork to use digitally, or you can recreate it on watercolor paper and put it in a special frame.

GALAXY EFFECT LETTERING

We're going to create our galaxy lettering by blending together a few specific marker colors for the letter background, and then adding stars with a white gel pen. The first few steps are going to be the same as your watercolor technique, so it should feel familiar (you can always go back to Chapter 6 [page 40] to refresh your memory if you need to).

STEP 1

Color onto a nonabsorbent surface with the following marker colors—dark blue, dark purple and magenta.

Remember, your nonabsorbent surface can be a baggie, something laminated or a plastic palette. As you experiment with this, you can try adding in other shades of blues and purples, or even black.

STEP 2

Dip the tip of your water brush pen into one or two of the colors.

Make sure the barrel of the pen is full. Water pens don't work without water!

STEP 3

Begin forming the letter using the brush lettering technique we learned in Chapter 17 (page 116).

Keep the pressure light as you form the upstroke, and then press down on the brush as you start moving it downward. Lighten the pressure again as you go back up toward the next letter.

STEP 4

Continue writing the word *love*, reloading your brush with different mixtures of colors as you go.

Remember, the brush is self-cleaning, so no matter how much mixing you do, it will eventually run clear.

STEP 5

Wait a couple of minutes for your letters to dry completely, and then go back with a white gel pen and draw tiny dots and stars on top.

If you have metallic gold and silver gel pens, you can use those too for some of the stars. To create my stars, I drew several intersecting lines, but you can also do five-pointed stars, if you prefer.

This galaxy technique also works really well for coloring in space-themed shapes like moons and large stars. Just draw the outline using a non-water-based marker, and then load your water brush with color and fill in the white space inside. When it's dry, add your embellishments.

Practice makes progress, so take some time to play around with this on the next page. If you decide to do more practicing in a sketchbook or on separate paper, you'll want to use hot-press watercolor paper for the best results. When you're ready, pencil in your design on the border page (don't forget your horizontal guidelines too) and get to work coloring it in. I decided to use the galaxy effect lettering for the most important words—*love you*, *moon* and *back*—and Funky Print Font (page 22) for *to the*, but you can vary the fonts for whatever parts of the quote you choose. This design also uses the ampersand you just learned how to create in Chapter 18 (page 123). Choose your favorite style and put it to use here. Don't forget that you can also color in the border!

PRACTICE BELOW

TWENTY

LETTERING NUMBERS

All of us have goals. Some are short-term, like getting a good grade on the next math test, learning a new hand lettering style or scoring a goal in this week's soccer game. Other goals take longer, like earning a black belt or making honor roll all year. No matter what the goal, though, the key to reaching it is to start taking steps right now! It's easy to put things off until someday, but that doesn't get us any closer to our goals. Instead, we need to get to work now. Whether it's studying for a test, practicing a sport or working on a skill we want to develop, we need to make it happen. We can wish and hope for someday to come, or we can start putting in the effort today. Only one of those choices will get us to where we want to be. What is one thing you can do today that will get you closer to reaching a goal?

By now, you've learned a variety of different fonts for creating hand lettered designs. You know how to write the alphabet in Faux Calligraphy Script and Print, Funky Print Font, Polka Dot–Filled Alphabet and Comic Book Print. Plus you know how to do floral letters and brush lettering. But there's more to this form of art than just letters. In this chapter we're going to take a look at how to create artistic numbers. Then you'll be able to write important dates on your calendar, jazz up your papers at school and decorate your planner or agenda even more than you already have.

LETTERING NUMBERS

Since you've already mastered these writing styles for letters, it's going to be a piece of cake to apply them to numbers. For each style, we will follow the same steps to create our numerals as we did for our letters. Here's how 0 through 9 will look in each font.

FAUX CALLIGRAPHY SCRIPT, FAUX CALLIGRAPHY PRINT & BRUSH LETTERING

1234567890

FUNKY PRINT

1234567890

POLKA DOT–FILLED ALPHABET

1234567890

FLORAL LETTERS

1234567890

COMIC BOOK PRINT

1234567890

See? Easy peasy! Practice writing some numerals in the space on the next page in your favorite styles. Try combining words and numbers too, like writing your birthday or today's date. Our focus in the lettered quote is the number 7; choose your favorite font for it and sketch your quote in pencil on the border page. My sample design uses the Polka Dot–Filled Alphabet (page 46) for the number and a combination of Comic Book Print (page 81) and Brush Lettering (page 116) for the rest of the words. I wrote all of the words in black, then used the watercolor technique (page 40) to fill in the open space in the 7. I added white polka dots with my gel pen once the color was dry. To embellish the rest of the quote, I drew a banner (page 52) around the word *someday* and colored it in with the watercolor technique. Make sure you write in a non-water-based marker, or your word will smear when the water pen touches it. If you don't have one, create the banner first and write on top of it when it's completely dry. Finally, I added a few small swirls (page 17) and teardrop shapes on both sides of the banner.

PRACTICE BELOW

This page is a decorative border made up of hand-lettered days of the week and numbers arranged around the edges. The center is blank.

2 TUESDAY sunday FRIDAY 4 monday 5
WEDNESDAY 6 3 thursday 3 7 SATURDAY WEDNESDAY 6

Right edge (top to bottom):
TUESDAY sunday FRIDAY 3 monday 4
1 2 thursday 5 3 WEDNESDAY

Bottom edge:
SATURDAY TUESDAY sunday FRIDAY 1 thursday 3 2 monday 4 WEDNESDAY SATURDAY TUESDAY

Left edge (top to bottom):
WEDNESDAY TURDAY monday FRIDAY thursday 7 FRIDAY 6 sunday TUESDAY SATURDAY

TWENTY-ONE

LET'S MAKE IT

Five Easy Project Ideas

Now that you've learned the basics of hand lettering, as well as some doodles and embellishments to make your designs pop, it's time to talk about where you can use your new skills. If you're like me, you'll suddenly find yourself wanting to letter everything. The great news is that, with the right supplies, you really can letter on just about anything, personalizing it and making it fabulous. Here are a few easy project ideas to get you started.

DIY WOODEN WALL SIGN

It's easy to add a personal touch to your room with a handmade sign. These also make great gifts for family members and friends! Wooden signs come in all shapes and sizes, so you can choose whatever works best for the space where you want to display it. You can find all of the supplies for this project at your local craft store as well as the craft section of retail stores like Walmart and Target.

MATERIALS

- Acrylic paint

- Paintbrush

- An unfinished wooden sign, any size and shape

- Paint pens or permanent markers

- Pencil with eraser

- Ruler (optional)

- Materials for hanging your sign, such as nails, a hammer and string

STEP 1

Paint the surface of your wooden sign any color you like.

Keep in mind that if you use a dark color, you'll want to write with white or metallic paint pens so it's visible on the dark color. If you want a chalkboard effect, you can paint the wood black and use a white paint pen for your lettering. Let the base coat dry completely before you move on to the next step.

STEP 2

After the paint is dry, use a pencil to sketch words and doodles on the sign.

If you want your lettering to be totally straight, you can lightly pencil in guidelines using a ruler. You can write your name, a favorite quote or anything else you want on your sign, including any of the designs you've created in this book. For my sample, I use Faux Calligraphy Script (page 11) with flower embellishments (page 60) in the corners, but you can do anything you can imagine.

STEP 3

Trace over your pencil lines with paint pens or permanent markers.

I prefer the look of the paint, but if all you have is a Sharpie®, it will do the trick. Because paint markers don't come with a brush tip, you'll need to use the Faux Calligraphy Script if you want the look of brush lettering.

STEP 4

After your words and doodles are totally dry, go back and erase any pencil marks you can still see.

Be sure to wait at least an hour so that you don't accidentally smear your design.

STEP 5

Display your sign for everyone to see!

If your sign comes with a string, bracket or nail hole already in place, all you have to do is hang it from an existing nail in the wall. If not, you'll want to ask a parent to help you attach some type of hardware to the back of the sign or hammer a nail into the wall where you want to hang it. You can also try using a mounting adhesive if you want to avoid nail holes in the wall.

HANDMADE CARDS

Anytime you give a card to someone, it's sure to brighten their day. Imagine how much your family and friends will enjoy receiving cards you've created by hand. These are simple to make, totally personal and much cheaper than buying cards in the store.

MATERIALS

- Scissors or a paper cutter

- 8½ x 11-inch (21.5 x 28-cm) white cardstock or hot-press watercolor paper (or any color you like)

- Pencil with eraser

- Your favorite lettering markers and pens

STEP 1

Cut your cardstock in half so that you have two pieces that are 5½ x 8½ inches (14 x 21.5 cm). One sheet of cardstock will make two cards.

STEP 2

Fold the cardstock pieces in half so that you have two cards that are 4¼ x 5½ inches (11 x 14 cm) on both sides.

STEP 3

Use a pencil to sketch your design on the front of the card.

The fold should be either on top or to the left, depending on whether you have a vertical or horizontal design. My sample card uses a banner (page 52), some simple swirls (page 17), Funky Print Font (page 22), Faux Calligraphy Script (page 11) and Brush Lettering (page 116). Many of the designs you created in this book, like Adventure Awaits (page 40) and Love You to the Moon & Back (page 129), would make great cards for all kinds of occasions.

STEP 4

Use your markers to create and color the design.

I recommend white cardstock so any and all colors look their best. If you prefer a different color, keep in mind how other colors will show up on it. If you plan on using the watercolor technique, you can use hot-press watercolor paper for your card instead.

STEP 5

Carefully erase any remaining pencil marks.

STEP 6

Share your card with a friend or family member! Don't forget to decorate the envelope too!

DIY PILLOW

Throw pillows are a great way to personalize your room. Now you can use your lettering skills to create a pillow that says anything you want! Use your favorite design from the chapters in this book or letter a quote that means something special to you. A monogram works well too, along with some of the swirls, flowers or other embellishments you've learned to draw. This project does require a bit of sewing, so you might want to get some help from an adult, if you're not sure how to do that part on your own.

MATERIALS

- Pencil with eraser

- Light-colored fabric cut into two 12½ x 12½-inch (32 x 32-cm) squares

- Fabric markers or fabric paint and paintbrushes

- Paper bag or newspaper

- Straight pins

- Thread and needle or sewing machine

- Polyester fiber fill

STEP 1

Use a pencil to sketch whatever design you like on one of your fabric squares. This will become the front of your pillow.

If you'd like to decorate the back too, you can sketch something on the other square as well. Be sure to leave at least a 1-inch (2.5-cm) border of the fabric undecorated. In my examples, I used Faux Calligraphy Script (page 11) along with simple embellishments like a heart and clouds. You can make your designs as basic or complex as you like. The Chase Your Dreams design you created in Chapter 14 (page 96) would be an awesome choice for a pillow.

STEP 2

Place newspaper or a paper bag under your fabric square to protect your work surface.

Color your design using fabric markers or fabric paint. Make sure your artwork is completely dry, and then erase any visible pencil lines.

STEP 3

Turn your decorated fabric square facedown and lay it on top of the other piece of fabric.

If you created designs on both pieces, the designs should be touching each other. Pin the two pieces of fabric together around the edges to hold them in place.

STEP 4

Sew around the edges of your fabric, leaving a 3-inch (7.5-cm) opening on the bottom edge.

If you are using a sewing machine, you'll want to make a 1¼-inch (3.2-cm) seam.

STEP 5

Using the 3-inch (7.5-cm) opening, turn your pillow right side out.

STEP 6

Fill your pillow with polyester fiber fill. You can use as much or as little as you like, depending on how squishy you want the pillow to be.

STEP 7

Hand stitch the 3-inch (7.5-cm) opening shut to hold the polyester fiber fill inside. Now your pillow is ready to use!

HAND LETTERED BINDER

Lettering can make even your schoolwork more interesting! Not only can you use some of your new skills when you're taking notes in class, you can also decorate your binders and notebooks any way you like.

MATERIALS

- Pencil with eraser

- A plain three-ring binder, any color

- Paint or permanent markers

- A clear-drying adhesive sealer, such as Mod Podge® or spray sealer (optional)

STEP 1

Sketch your design in pencil on your binder.

You can illustrate the name of the subject you'll be using it for or just create something that inspires you. In my example, I wrote "Math" in Polka Dot–Filled Alphabet (page 46), and then added numbers along the bottom in Comic Book Print (page 81). I drew a plus sign, and then added swirly embellishments (page 17) along the binder's edge.

STEP 2

Go over your design with paint or permanent markers.

STEP 3

If you used paint markers, you may want to use a spray sealer or give the binder a coat of clear-drying adhesive sealer, such as Mod Podge®, so that the paint won't come off with normal wear and tear. Permanent marker should hold up well no matter how much you use your binder.

If you think you might want to rotate through new designs during the school year, a less permanent option is to purchase a binder with clear plastic pockets on the outside. Then you can create designs on sketch paper instead and just slide them in and out whenever you like.

LETTERED JEWELRY DISH

Anyone who has jewelry knows you need a place to keep it when it's not being worn. A personalized jewelry dish is a fun project to create, and it's useful too, because it can hold rings, earrings and even necklaces until you're ready to wear them. Make one for yourself or create one as a gift for your mom, grandma or friend.

MATERIALS

- A small plain-colored dish (you can often find one at thrift stores or yard sales)

- Rubbing alcohol

- Paper towel

- Paint markers or ceramic markers

STEP 1

Clean the surface of your jewelry dish with rubbing alcohol.

STEP 2

Create a design using your paint markers.

We won't be able to sketch in pencil this time, because pencil won't write on glass or ceramic, but you can always trace your dish onto a piece of paper and do a rough copy first if you want to practice. My sample designs are a simple monogram in Faux Calligraphy Script (page 11) with some dots to embellish, and the phrase "shine bright" in a combination of Faux Calligraphy Script and Funky Print Font (page 22).

STEP 3

If you used paint markers, let your dish sit and cure for 72 hours before using it. If you used ceramic markers, follow the instructions on the marker packaging.

STEP 4

Put your dish to use or give it as a gift!

You can also decorate regular plates and cups, but keep in mind that even if they are labeled nontoxic, paint pens are not food safe. Some brands of ceramic markers are food safe, but check the packaging carefully to make sure before eating off a painted surface. If you're decorating a mug or glass, all paint should be at least 1 inch (2.5 cm) from the rim. Better safe than sick!

MORE LETTERING PROJECT IDEAS

The project ideas and tutorials in this chapter are just a few of the many things you can create using hand lettering. Here's a list of more project ideas you can try:

- Aprons
- Bible journals
- Book covers
- Bookmarks
- Canisters
- Canvases
- Chalkboard signs
- Christmas ornaments
- Coasters
- Coffee mugs
- Coloring pages
- Gift tags
- Journals
- Maps
- Notes
- Notebooks
- Picture frames
- Plates
- Tote bags
- Travel mugs
- Treat bags
- T-shirts
- Wall art
- Windows
- Wooden trays, crates, etc.
- Wood slices

For more inspiration and step-by-step instructions for lettering projects like these, be sure to visit www.oneartsymama.com/lettering-projects.

ACKNOWLEDGMENTS

Writing a book is a lot of work. Illustrating a book takes a lot of time and effort. Doing both means I needed a village to support me. Heartfelt thanks to the following people for making this project possible:

Will, Sarah, Meg and the Page Street Publishing Team—Thank you for believing in me the first time around and for jumping on board so quickly when I tossed the idea for a kids' book your way. This book wouldn't exist without you. Literally.

Dan—Thank you for your constant support, encouragement and love, especially when I decided to write a book while we were adopting with a deadline during the holidays. Go Team Latta!

Noah—Thank you for understanding when Mama needed to work instead of play and for constantly inspiring me with your creativity. You have so many awesome ideas, and I can't wait to see what you do with this book.

Nathan—I am so lucky and blessed to be your mama. Thank you for adding so much love and laughter to my life. You are the bravest person I know.

Mom & Dad—You always said I could do anything if I put my mind to it. Thank you for teaching me to create and for always letting me pursue my love of art.

Erin—Thank you for being the sister God gave to me and for holding down the fort at One Artsy Mama while I was busily writing this book. Every short girl needs a tall best friend, and I'm awfully glad you're mine.

Zoey, Rose and Paris—Thank you for sharing your ideas and feedback with me as I planned this book. It wouldn't be the same without you, and I hope you love how it turned out. This one's for you, and I can't wait to see what you create!

Jennifer Fitzpatrick of Full Heart Photography—Thanks for your beautiful work.

Readers of *Hand Lettering for Relaxation*—From the bottom of my heart, thank you for your overwhelming support and response to my first book. Because of you, it has already gone to print three times in less than six months and has been a success beyond my wildest dreams. Because of you, there was a chance for a second book, and let's hope a third and a fourth....

ABOUT THE AUTHOR

Amy Latta is an artist, blogger and author of the bestselling book *Hand Lettering for Relaxation*. Her original hand lettered designs have been featured nationally in Starbucks and GAP stores, and her first book has received international acclaim in its Portuguese version titled *Caligrafia para Relaxar*. In addition to inspiring her online community, Amy teaches workshops both locally and at conferences across the United States. As a former middle and high school teacher and the mama of two boys, Amy is an expert at working with kids and loves sharing her knowledge of lettering with them. You can learn more about Amy and her creative endeavors at www.oneartsymama.com.

INDEX